mommy's hair is everywhere

Written by
Jessica Danias

Illustrated by
Summer Nguyen

Written by Jessica Danias
Illustrated by Summer Nguyen

For my baby Cole,
without you my hair would not be everywhere.

-- J.D.

To my beloved friends and family,
thank you for believing in me as an artist.

-- S.N.

Mommy's hair is not just on her head
She finds it every morning in her bed.

Oh!

She finds her hair every hour
She even finds it in the shower.

Mommy thought she found a bug.
Don't worry, it's just her hair on the rug.

She finds her hair in the living room
Now it's time to grab the vacuum.

Mommy's hair is in the nursery
But she didn't find it purposely.

She found her hair in the baby's crib
Some may think that it's just a fib.

Mommy finds her hair on dad

But he finds it funny and will never get mad.

Mommy's hair loss seems ongoing
Finding it everywhere is very annoying.

Post-baby hair loss is a real struggle
The amount that is lost is not so subtle.

No worries mommy, don't get appalled.
Even when you think that you might go bald.

No reason to feel so insecure
You are still beautiful in every way for sure.

The excessive hair shedding is just a phase
Pretty soon you will see better days.

blessed

traveler

author

mother

nurse

wife

thankful

So forget what's happening right above
And remember to enjoy what's there to love.

Daddy and baby will love you regardless of your hairstyle
They just care about seeing your beautiful smile.

Your gorgeous hair will always grow back
It's just your hormones out of whack.

So in the meantime just keep brushing your hair,
That way you won't keep finding it everywhere.

Jessica Danias is a first-generation Chinese American born and raised in Michigan. She graduated from the University of Detroit Mercy with a Bachelor of Science in Nursing. She has worked as a nurse for almost ten years. *Mommy's Hair Is Everywhere* is Jessica's first self-published book inspired by her own experiences of motherhood. She currently resides in Fort Wayne, Indiana with her husband and baby boy. You can follow her at @jessica.danias.

Summer Nguyen is a college student by day, comic artist by night. She is a senior at the University of Michigan with a degree in Information Science and a minor in Asian Studies. Besides creating art, she loves to explore new places with friends, read, or spend time outdoors. This book is her first major illustrative project and she is excited for more! You can find her online at @ssummering.

www.ingramcontent.com/pod-product-compliance
Lightning Source LLC
LaVergne TN
LVHW072131070426
835513LV00002B/59